How I
Was Able to Eat Once A
Week

by

Brother Joe Muhammad

Follower of The Honorable Elijah Muhammad

to Bro Dewayne
Muhammad
From Bro Joe Muhammad
May Allah Bless you
2/22/18
347-258-2991

ISBN-13: 978-0615616070
ISBN-10: 0615616070

Cover design created by Brother Raymond Muhammad (2X)

Cover Photo by Michael Morris

Additional Photos by Sister Arnise Muhammad

How I
Was Able to Eat Once A Week

by
Brother Joe Muhammad

Follower of The Honorable Elijah Muhammad

Word of Mouth Book Publications

Jersey City NJ

Giving Birth to the Best Books on Earth!

www.wombpublications.com

Email: yourbrotherjoe@yahoo.com

With These Hands of Allah
New York, NY

Website: www.withthesehandsofallah.com

Brother Joe Muhammad

"We are the God of ourselves and we can make a habit of eating once every seven (7) days. We can train our bodies not to desire to take food, until the end of the seven (7) day period. We are just what we make of ourselves".

The Honorable Elijah Muhammad

How to Eat to Live Book 2   pg. 15

Foreword

In the Name of Allah the Beneficent the Merciful

Words seem inadequate to express how grateful I am for Allah coming in the person of Master Fard Muhammad and I can never thank Him enough for blessing us with the Most Honorable Elijah Muhammad and I thank them both for giving to us an extension of grace and mercy in the The Honorable Minister Louis Farrakhan.

Helping Brother Joe transfer his thoughts to paper made me feel like a birthing coach assisting a woman bringing a newborn baby into the world. It was truly a labor of love. I feel deeply honored and blessed to have been a part of this historic endeavor. After listening to him express his desire to write the book of his journey to eating once a week, then to begin writing the book and actually *see* it come to life, I can say I'm a witness to a god saying **Be** and it **Is**. Brother Joe has an amazing ability to tell a story in such a way as to make you feel every word as if you were actually there when it was taking place. I found myself laughing, crying, hanging at the edge of my seat all while trying not to miss a beat on the keyboard. It is an experience I shall never forget and will treasure for the rest of my life.

-Sister Arnice Muhammad

Table of Contents

Page

Acknowlegements.. iii

Preface... iv

Introduction:... v

Chapter One: The Journey 1

Chapter Two: Can't Eat One Meal A Day 3

Chapter Three: 2 days and 3 days a week Scientists.... 7

Chapter Four: Catching "The Glow"............................ 11

Chapter Five: Methuselah Who!..................... 13

Chapter Six: Joining "The Nation"............................. 15

Chapter Seven: Meeting another "Food Scientist........ 16

Chapter Eight: A New Fast.................................... 18

Chapter Nine: The Reward........................... 20

Chapter Ten: The Road To One Meal A Week 21

Chapter Eleven: Let Me Explain............................. 22

Chapter Twelve: Divine Inspiration........................... 24

Chapter Thirteen: Prayer is First 26

Chapter Fourteen: The Glow................................... 28

Table of Contents

(cont'd)

Page

Chapter Fifteen: Doubt, then Confidence 30

Chapter Sixteen: Remember the 21 day Fast 33

Chapter Seventeen: 1975: The Separation.................... 36

Chapter Eighteen: Captain Yusuf Shah's Guidance....... 39

Chapter Nineteen: One Day a Week Journey 41

Chapter Twenty: Food God.................................... 44

Chapter Twenty One: No Joke.............................. 47

Chapter Twenty Two: Capt. Shah: It's the Glow Brother   50

Chapter Twenty Three: Capt. Shah: Science of Drilling   53

Chapter Twenty Four: What I Learn, I Share 55

Chapter Twenty Five: We Dig our Graves w/our Teeth.   58

Chapter Twenty Six: Wisdom.................................. 60

Conclusion: 61

Acknowledgements

In The Name of Allah the Beneficent the Merciful

First of all I want to give thanks to Almighty God Allah for coming in the person of Master Fard Muhammad, and for blessing us with such a divine man, The Most Honorable Elijah Muhammad, and when he was no longer in our midst, I give special thanks to them both for leaving us a reminder, comforter and guide in The Honorable Minister Louis Farrakhan.

Thanks to my family for all of their love and support. Thank you to all of my brothers and sisters throughout The Nation; and to all of the beautiful brothers and sisters I have been blessed to know across the world.

Very special thanks to my business partner, Sister Arnise Muhammad, for her typing skills and unwavering dedication.

And to Brother Leroy Muhammad (23X) for editing and proofreading. Thank you for your confidence in me and for foreseeing the vision, brother.

And to my Brother Raymond Muhammad (2x) from Jersey City, NJ, for his editorial and publishing input, and for ultimately wrapping up and putting a period to this project.

Preface

In The Name of Allah the Beneficent the Merciful

Being in the company of those who were present when the Honorable Elijah Muhammad was in our midst is a great privilege, and can be very rewarding. There are things that the pioneers and trailblazers experienced in their time of Nation building that many of us sit back and marvel at, because when you give ear to our history, it is such a beautiful history, and no one can tell it better than those who were there. Brother Joe Muhammad is one of those brothers, and after meeting him for just a few minutes, he will impact you with something of himself and of the teachings that is certain to last you for a liftetime.

Sometimes we are guilty of not having patience with each other because of our newfound wisdom. We are all so eager to get our point across that we fail to listen *first*. While compiling and preparing these pages for print, I had an opportunity to really **listen** to what this brother is saying, and also took notice of his unorthodox style of speech, and at times I literally thought I was reading the words of The Honorable Elijah Muhammad!

Brother Joe has a unique way with words that proves to make him a stone of stumbling for many; you may find yourself underestimating the truth coming from brothers' mouth if you just listen to **how** he says a thing, and not to **what** he's actually trying to say. On these pages you are about to read is a testament to what is laying on our brother's heart, so I humbly ask us all to lend our ear to our brother. Let us **hear** him.

Raymond Muhammad - **Editor**

Introduction

I hate to see the condition that our people are in with so many illnesses such as heart disease, diabetes, and high blood pressure. We suffer so much from not knowing what to eat and how to eat properly.

After reading "How to Eat to Live", there's so much in the book. Listening to me and my experience is just one persons observation and testimony, but to read it for yourself, and applying it to yourself is where the real benefits and blessings are.

Out of all the books that I've read "How to Eat to Live" was the most influential because it teaches how to expand your life by eating properly, and we all want to live long lives.

So I want to encourage my people to get the book "How to Eat to Live" Book 1 and Book 2. It is the essence in both these books that motivated me to write this book.

Joe Muhammad – **Author**

In the Name of Allah

And

In the Name of His Messenger

Chapter One

The Journey

Let me tell you a story about the summer of 1971. My curiosity was about to take me on a journey I never would have believed. It would be a journey of self-discipline and self- improvement, and would testify to a basic truth which is; whenever someone achieves anything great they have to first follow in someone else's path. Whether good or bad, they had to follow someone.

I was always curious and fascinated by how the Nation of Islam Muslims looked. "Why was their skin so beautiful," I would always ask myself. I actually thought it was grease, but what brand was it? I wanted that look, so this particular summer day I approached this Muslim brother and asked him, "What kind of grease do you use?"

His response was at first a smile that turned into a laugh. But his smile was so bright that I had to smile and laugh with him, but I still was waiting for his answer. I said to him, "Okay my brother, enough of the laugh, can you please tell me the secret?"

Still smiling, but with a serious tone, he said, "Technically it's not really a secret. I'm a follower of the Honorable Elijah Muhammad. He has written several books and one of them is "How to Eat to Live", and now since you are curious, I'll share with you what I've learned from it. I would advise you to get the book".

He began, "First of all, you asked the question what grease do I use and I take that as a compliment because it's not grease, it's a glow you're seeing." Then he dropped a few lessons on me from "How to Eat to Live". The first was that Muslims were supposed to eat once a day. Oh by the way, I have to tell you that this conversation took place in a prison yard, we were incarcerated. When you are confined, you see meals as a privilege that can't be denied you. You can enjoy yourself at least three times a day, so when he hit me with this one meal a day, I didn't wanna give up no privileges but I wanted to get this glow! This was for me a personal challenge. I thought to myself that if the Muslims were stepping back from meals, this was way tougher than doing bunches of pushups.

Chapter Two
Can't Eat One Meal A Day

I still loved to eat so I began to eat two meals a day. What helped me was that he gave me a "How to Eat to Live" book. His name was Brother John, and I began to eavesdrop on his conversations. He not only had a beautiful glow, he had a beautiful personality and he was one of the kindest brothers that I ever met. He was humble, able to tolerate much and he shared a great deal of time teaching me about Islam. He had a perfect way of correcting me when I was out of order. By the way he treated me, it made me want to become a Muslim. So one day, as if he was a psychic, he asked me, "When are you going to come to be a Muslim?" My answer to his question was, "When I stop smoking my herb and making my wine I think I'll be ready." To Brother John, my response, my answer, my excuse, or my bail out was unacceptable.

His words were to me: "First, let's get something straight brother. I'm trying to welcome you to Muhammad's emergency ward. Second of all, I'm also in the emergency ward, I'm getting my treatment too. Just because I graduated out of process class I'm still processing till the day I die.

There's always room for improvement." He said to me, "You are a beautiful brother, Brother Joe; we would love to have you. You are loved by so many people. I appreciate your compliment on my spirit in my trying to help you, but first of all let me tell you that when you stand up, the law of Islam, the restrictive law is in full effect." He turned and looked at me straight and said, "Brother Joe when you go to the hospital do you wait till you get well to go the hospital?" I said, "Why would I do that? I go to the hospital because I'm sick." So he said "That's why I'm asking you to come with all the problems you got because I'm welcoming you to Muhammad's hospital. That's why we have books like "Message to the Blackman", "Fall of America", "How to Eat to Live", "Our Saviour Has Arrived" and "The Holy Quran". These books can help you with so much that have to do with life. My favorite book is "How to Eat to Live."

One morning I was going to get my toast, jelly and eggs and the brother said, "Wait a minute Brother Joe, you gonna have to begin to eat twice a day." I said, "Can I wait till later? Can I start next week?" His response was, "No sir!" To be honest, I wasn't feeling that at all. But as I watched the Muslim

4

brothers get their juice, I got mine. That's when my discipline started to set in, however, watching the other inmates all around me eat their food, I'm not gonna tell a lie, I was very disappointed.

One day at breakfast as I was drinking my juice, I heard a group of brothers having a debate. One of the brothers said that the Honorable Elijah Muhammad chewed 30 times before swallowing. Then, the other brother responded, "No it was 25". Then another brother responded and said, "No, it was 23 times." Then the other brother said, "You act like you was there and he told you!" So I guess in my interest in what they were talking about, my curiosity kicked in again, I said, "Excuse me." They said, "Yes Brother Joe? I asked, "Why did he chew so many times?" One of the brothers said, "Brother Joe you ain't got nothing to do with this conversation, you stick with tryin to eat once a day."

Then the other brother responded, "The brothers' tryin to learn, don't ever talk to him like that again!" So then the brother went on to explain to me, "You know baby food is all crushed up; so when we get table food you take two bites and you swallow it and it goes directly into your system. That's why we must chew several times before we swallow so the food can digest better." After listening to that conversation, I didn't even have an appetite at lunch time. It was one of the strangest things because that day at lunch they were serving one of the favorite meals to eat when you were incarcerated - half chicken with rice and beans.

Chapter Three

<u>2 Days A Week, 3 Days A Week Scientists</u>

As several months passed, they had a brother come in and he was already an FOI (Fruit of Islam). His skin looked clear, he ate every three days. In other words, he ate twice a week. Then there also at the time was another brother that ate every other day. That means he ate three days out of the week. He was slim and that also put my antennas up to ask more questions. We were already eating only once a day so I wanted to know the reason why they ate every other day and every three days; So one day I happened to approach the brothers and it was like a blessing cause they both were together. I said, "Excuse me, do you mind if I ask some questions?" Looking at each of them I said, "Why do *you* eat every other day and why do *you* eat every three days?" Please forgive me for not mentioning their names I can't remember them at this time.

They both smiled at me at the same time and one said "Who's gonna go first?" Then the other one said, "Since I eat every other day and you eat every three days, I'll go first and you go behind me."

He began by saying, "I figure with the teachings of How to Eat to Live, you first learn to eat once a day. It's like you're a runner. If I run a mile, I then move up to another mile; I wanted to get stronger in my dietary law so I ate every other day; so my response was "How did it feel? Was it hard? Was it easy?" He said, "It was kind of difficult because my body was asking for food every day. It was a little hard at first because I had to eat every other day. It's just like you do 25 push ups and then up it to 30 push ups. After difficulty comes ease."

So the question I asked was very interesting to me and I'm trying to process the answer. As I'm listening hard, the other brother who ate every three days cuts into the first brother's answer with, "Are you finished?" The response was, "Yes sir brother!" Then the second brother jumps right in and says "Now let me explain how I am able to eat every 3 days." I was shaking my head saying,"Brother can you please let me digest *this*?" I was listening to two food scientists!

After listening to the first brother I wanted to say that's enough for the day but the brother that ate every three days looked so anxious with his beautiful smile I just had to hear what he had to say.

He started by saying, "When I ate every other day I felt beautiful. I felt open. I felt so open it was as though I could see through people. So after several weeks or months, Brother Joe, I just felt I wanted to go to the next stage. So what I did was I put the thought in my mind that it wasn't going to be easy. The times I was supposed to eat, I was having breakdowns already, so I went into praying and prayers brought ease and Allah guided me through to be successful. You must understand, Brother Joe, The Honorable Elijah Muhammad described eating times from four to six, and you begin to understand why. Your stomach is so small you can't fit all the food at one time, so you have to try to eat 4 o'clock sharp. Even though you're incarcerated, you have to put something in and take advantage of your two hour eating time. At first I misunderstood the four to six, but I finally figured out that for me eating every three days, those were my eating hours." He continued, "Whenever I ate on time, and by having the knowledge that my stomach had shrunk; whatever I put in it made me full, and it seemed like my body would eat that up within a half hour. I could then put a little more in it." I then interrupted saying, "But brother you're supposed to eat *once* a day." The brother's response was, "You don't know how difficult this is when you go to eat every other day. You think that you can eat a lot when it's time to eat, but you come to realize that you have a smaller belly. In other words, your belly doesn't ask for that much more. Brother Joe tomorrow's another day, we'll talk more tomorrow."

Chapter Four

<u>Catching "The Glow"</u>

After listening to both of these brothers I was now pissy drunk. What I mean by this is when I went back to my cell, I now thought I could go ahead and eat every other day, and I had only just started out. When it came time for me to eat dinner that night I walked over to where they were sitting and told my brothers, "I'm not going to eat dinner, I'm going on every other day." They just smiled and, here we go again, their beautiful smile turned into a laugh and I asked the brothers, "Do you think that's funny?" One brother responded, "You are so determined and so wonderful, Brother Joe, but we don't want you to rush into it like that, so please, Brother Joe eat your food." So I listened to my brother and I went back to get my plate and sat down with them.

As I was eating I was smiling and the brother said to me, "You've got so much fire in you." He then looked past me and spoke to the other brother and said, "This brother might be ready for something, we don't know. We both might be underestimating him. Even though he's new at this, he's such a fast learner and his interest is looking so good. He's even glowing more than us!" Then the other brother said, "The strange part about it is that he's out-glowing us, and we're eating every other day and every three days." So I started smiling with joy after hearing those words from them and it seemed like at the same time they both said, "Look at him, see what I mean." I was just smiling and smiling. I said, "Now y'all starting to confuse me." The brother just looked and said," Allah works in mysterious ways. Good night Brother Joe. Tomorrow we're gonna get into some deep science."

Chapter Five
Methuselah Who?!

That night I could not sleep because my mind was wondering what was gonna be said tomorrow. Just that thought alone kept me up, because I couldn't get them off my mind. I was learning so much that the knowledge, wisdom, and understanding was keeping me up. The next day came and I *walked* over to him, but it felt more like I *ran*. We always had our learning circle. What I loved about it was we were always building and there wasn't that much temptation in incarceration. So I was able to focus more, due to the fact that we were incarcerated. I went to the brother and said "I'm ready," but little did I know I was not ready.

He said, "Are you ready for this, Brother Joe?" I shook my head and said "I don't think so", as if I knew he was gonna say something that I never thought of, or heard of. What came out next was, "Have you ever heard of Methuselah?" I shook my head, "No sir." He said, "Methuselah ate every 17 days." I guess those of you reading this, you don't have to ask me my response. You can judge it by imagining if somebody told *you* that. If hearing brothers teaching me on eating every other day and every three days was dizzying, imagine them taking it up seventeen more notches! When he told me Methuselah lived to nearly 866 years I guess I could understand that because a man with that kind of will power can live a long time. I'm sharing all of this with you so you have a better understanding of how I ever even got the *thought* to want to eat once a week!

Chapter Six

<u>Joining "The Nation"</u>

My curiosity had brought me into the orbit of the Muslims. I can now understand the warning of people outside the Nation, "Don't go near them. They will change you." That warning is a crazy kind of warning, one that keeps all the crabs in the pot while someone is turning up the heat, and tryna kill all of 'em'. The orbit of the Muslims is knowledge, science and just plain common sense. It's common sense for us not to wear out our stomachs, clog our arteries, jam our pancreas, kidneys, liver and slow our thinking down by stuffing our mouths and stomachs with food and drink.

The knowledge the FOI dropped on me in prison drove me to formally join up at Temple #7D in the Bronx under the leadership of Brother James 7X and Minister Farrakhan was The National Representative of the Honorable Elijah Muhammad. When I was released from prison after a year, I was eating twice a week.

Chapter Seven

Meeting another "Food Scientist"

Everybody's life is filled with stories. When you are on a journey seeking knowledge, that very desire of seeking opens doors and brings you into contact with people who can help you complete your journey. So here's another story of meeting another "food scientist".

He was a brother from California who was a guest speaker at the Temple. His subject was "How to Eat to Live". Here I am, fresh out of incarceration where I was taught by some heavies, and Allah puts another one right in my path.

Here are some of the pearls of wisdom he dropped on us. He began by saying we might be eating once a day, or just two or three times a week, but that didn't mean we were eating right.

"Fried foods and meat will take you out of your discipline," he explained. "The majority of you look like Muslims who just got out of prison and haven't contaminated yourself with alcohol or drugs. You have that clear look. But you should be looking like that young fellow over there (he was pointing to me)."

A brother in the class shouted out that I was seventeen and the speaker called me to the front. He said, "For the first time I can see what The Honorable Elijah Muhammad said his program would do, and that is to make us look like a baby." After the lecture he and I spoke about better foods to eat. He said, "Your spirit is strengthened by eating right." He impressed me with his knowledge of foods. At that time I was eating twice a week. I would eat either Wednesday and Sunday or Thursday and Sunday. I would try to make it past Wednesday, but if I couldn't, I would eat on Wednesday. Remember, I had practice and the support of the brotherhood while I was incarcerated. I had that knowledge of how to do it, and lots of practice.

Chapter Eight

A New Fast

The brother from California introduced me to a cleansing fast. This was a new trial but I accepted the challenge. Here's how it works over a period of 21 days.

Days 1 and 2:	I consumed only water.
Days 3 and 4:	I ate fruit.
Days 5 and 6:	I ate vegetables.
Days 7 and 8:	I drank water
Days 9 and 10:	I ate fruit.
Days 11 and 12:	I ate vegetables.
Days 13 and 14:	I ate fruit.
Days 15 and 16:	I ate vegetables
Days 17 and 18:	I consumed only water.
Days 19 and 20:	I ate fruit.
21st Day:	I ate vegetables.

My experience during this fast was that the first two

days with water only was a major challenge. It was due to my being hooked on sweets, candy. I had to fight the urge to get me some candy in my mouth. The next challenge was the fact that no meat was in my diet during the 21 days, however, during the 5th and 6th days when I was eating vegetables, I began to feel better.

The California Brother (forgive me I do not remember his name) had explained the science of this fast as a cleansing one that removes old matter from the colon. With this fast, the body is cleansing itself. You can feel the organs moving stuff down and out. You supply the water and fruit which cleanses, while the vegetables are replacing some of your nutrients.

About the 12th day you can see self-improvement. The self-improvement feeds your discipline. What I mean is you can see the worth of the fast. Seeing is believing. Also, you want to keep dealing with the challenge because the prize is your bodys' cleansing out.

Chapter Nine

The Reward

What I felt during this fast was relaxation. I felt that I was cleansing myself of what had been harming me that I didn't realize – sweets, meat, and starches.

I also began to pick up on what people were thinking because it causes you to think more mathematical, and seeing through or understanding clearer what others were saying to me, even what they weren't saying. Your mind becomes clearer. Discipline pulls you closer to the God in you. That's why you are able to see people clearer and pick up on their thoughts. You're like an athlete doing super things, on a consistent basis. This comes after disciplining yourself.

After the 21 days I felt like a new man. I did it again three months later and it was rough because I had let too much time go between, but, I experienced a beautiful feeling that I can hardly describe; that's hard to put into words.

Chapter Ten

The Road To One Meal A Week

Now I will begin to explain to you all of the trials and tribulations that I went through to achieve the goal of eating one meal a week. We all have certain goals and ambitions that we strive to achieve in Islam. In 1994, my goal was to eat once every other day, and then to eat once every three days.

When I got to every three days, the urge to try came over me, and I wanted to eat every three days. Then I wanted to eat every two days and then the next time I would eat would be on the third day. We all like to experiment and I wanted to go higher, so I went to every four days, which meant that the next time I ate was on the third day.

Chapter Eleven

<u>Let Me Explain</u>

Consistently for three weeks to a month, I was on every three days, then every four days. Let me better explain it to you. If I ate on a Sunday, the next time I would eat was on a Thursday. Then I dropped back down, the next time I ate would be on Sunday, so that's what I mean when I say I ate every 4/3. One of the things I achieved out of that is I didn't sleep that much. I was mostly rested because I didn't have any solid foods in me. Food is a drug, so I was almost a master in the discipline of food. It's so much that I've experienced from eating properly. Your spirit is so aware that you are able to tolerate people better. You have a lot more patience, but you must remember since you're open, you're very vulnerable too. Your days go so peacefully, and you look at life as so much more beautiful, so I wondered how I would feel if I ate every five days, and every four days.

Again, I will explain. Let's start with Sunday. If I ate Sunday, the next time I would eat would be Friday. Then after Friday the next time I would eat would be on Tuesday; so right now I was on every five days and on every four days. I guess you're waiting for me to tell you what I experienced. At first it's not all that comfortable because you're still struggling, because you must remember the 4/3 that I was on for a while.

Whenever you go up to another level of eating you don't just land there, you work yourself there and then the comfort sets in. I guess you wonder whether I wanted to go to 6/5. No sir. I wanted to enjoy the blessing to be able to make it on this level for a while. You gotta remember everybody has goals in Islam. If you don't have a goal, you better find one of Allah's talents or gifts in yourself whether it's drilling, training, taking pictures, writing, computers, etc. and get busy doing something for yourself!

Chapter Twelve

Divine Inspiration

My goal was to practice eating properly. When I
worked out I had to be cautious not to overwork
myself. I was never able to see so much beauty in
people until I started learning how to discipline
myself on eating every 5 days and going up the
ladder. I thank Almighty God Allah for The Most
Honorable Elijah Muhammad to be able to write
such a book as "How to Eat to Live". Now I can
clearly understand some of the wisdom that The
Honorable Elijah Muhammad gave to us that we
could look 16 years old. You actually may not know
what I am talking about until you experience it
yourself. By experiencing it, you will see how your
thoughts get so clear and you don't think too much
of yourself. It's not saying that you're nobody, but
you humble yourself so much. It's like when you
listen to music... like the song "The Closer I get To
You...the more you make me see". When I listened
to that song I was actually thinking of Master Fard
Muhammad and The Honorable Elijah Muhammad.

It's almost like you're not in control of your life, its God that's guiding you. I can't leave out the Honorable Minister Louis Farrakhan. When the Nation was through, done with and everybody thought we were finished, I could clearly say all praise is due to Allah for giving us Minister Farrakhan, The Honorable Elijah Muhammad's National Representative. All praise is due to Allah. He is the one that got us back on track. I could never forget Minister Louis Farrakhan when he came up to Cornell University. I think it was about 1977 when he came. He was working to rebuild the Nation. He had no security. If it was not for me seeing him at Cornell University that year, I would have never picked "How to Eat to Live" back up again. All praise is due to Allah for The Honorable Elijah Muhammad and The Honorable Minister Louis Farrakhan.

Chapter Thirteen

Prayer Is First

I want to share with you what I got out of the Nation of Islam and "How to Eat to Live". We all have our minds as well as our imaginations. Now think about what The Honorable Elijah Muhammad said to the believers; that Master Fard Muhammad told him he would climb a mountain 40 miles high and eat rattlesnakes just to save one of us. Just that alone tells us what kind of love he has for us. One of the best things I could tell you to help your journey in Islam is to get the "Muslim Daily Prayers" book. It is a small book, but it is very powerful. On page 9 of the "Muslim Daily Prayers" book, it explains about Preparation for Prayer, and it states: "The Muslims' daily prayers are not to be taken for ordinary rituals. You must perform your prayers with utmost sincerity and seriousness, because they represent your communion with your Maker, Almighty Allah." A ritual is something we do as an everyday routine such as, "As Salaam Alaikum", "Good Morning", "Good Evening", etc. Always remember, the remembrance of Allah is the highest force. Learning how to eat properly is also a force, but focusing on Allah must come first.

I was focusing on Allah so much and my will power built up so strong that I stepped up to eating 6/5. What I mean is I would eat every six days and then every five days, then every six days and then every five days.   Then I began to understand what The Honorable Elijah Muhammad meant when he said "Set yourself in heaven at once." When trials and tribulations came my way, I was in such a peaceful state of mind.   What I'm sharing with you is whether you are eating once a day or every other day, when you better yourself it helps you in all areas of your life.

Chapter Fourteen

The Glow

By the time I moved on to eating every six days and then every five days, I was also working with the new brothers in the processing class. They were always asking me questions and would always say, "You have such a beautiful glow Brother Joe". When they found out I was eating every six and every five days they began to question me more, so I had what you might call a small reputation. The time came when I wanted to move onto the next level and wanted to go to 7/6 – eating every seven days, then every six days, then every seven days, then every six days.

It just so happened that the first day I decided to do it, I was already on the 6th day going on to the 7th day. The strange thing about it was that it was to be the completion day, and one of the processing brothers mentioned to the Student Minister that I was going to go to eating every 7 days. The Student Minister went on and started teaching his class. He happened to also be the History of Islam teacher for the processing class, and was always the second speaker to come on, while Brother Lieutenant was the first to speak and open up the class. I always took the new brothers out to train them on how to sell "The Final Call" newspaper.

Chapter Fifteen

Doubt, Then Confidence

On this particular day when the Student Minister began to teach he said something that broke my spirit to eat every seven days. My spirit was broken because he said that, "In this day and time you cannot eat once a week because there's so much going on in the world that it can't be done". That dampened my spirit so much that when I went home, I told my wife that it ain't no use in me going for eating every seven days because the Student Minister said you cannot do it in this day and time. My wife looked at me and smiled and she said, "The Minister cannot tell you that you can't eat once a week." My response was, "Yes, the Minister can tell me that." Then she said, "Well, according to what I read in "How to Eat to Live" you can eat once a week. Let me find it, I just read it in "How to Eat to Live". I'll show it to you." I said "What did you read?" I could not recall what part or page she was referring to. She said, "Just wait, and let me find it!" My wife pulled out the book, searched and found it. There it was:

"How to Eat to Live" Book Two on page 182:
"*Only eat one (1) meal a day and you will*

surely live long. Eat the proper food if you eat once, twice or three times a week. Do not say that you cannot eat once a week. It is the way that you train your stomach. You can make a habit of eating once every week and you will survive happily. So EAT TO LIVE and not to die."

It was right there so clearly, so much that I had forgot. So after reading that, I made up my mind. I would keep going and eat on Sunday. I would stay on my once a week drive, so when Sunday came to eat, I ate. When asked, I always said I ate once a week, not every 7 days. Much encouragement and compliments coming from many brothers and sisters saying that I was a god, a "baby food god," helped me to believe and strive. I don't want you to think that I'm trying to sound boastful. I give all thanks and praise to Almighty God Allah for The Honorable Elijah Muhammad, and we must clearly remember that Islam dignifies you, classifies you.

During the week I would go to the juice bar, but this was usually around the 3rd or 4th day during the week. It was never sooner than that. I would ask for celery, beets, carrots and I would watch him throw it in the juicer. Then I'd drink it so it would go to all parts of my body. It was filling. I know you want to ask me, "Did you get tempted to eat solid food?"

The answer is "No ma'am, No sir." When you get into the 3rd or 4th day it's more control up in your mind than in your body. If you ever strive to do this, once you experience it you'll know what I'm talking about. Discipline is an honor and being disciplined does not mean that you are being punished.

When I pick up the "Message to the Black Man" book and read where it says 'we are the strong, the wise, the best, but do not know it', eating once a week made me feel all three in one. I wouldn't know how to thank Allah for giving such divine wisdom, knowledge, and understanding of who we are, except to strive to live it to the best of my abilities.

Chapter Sixteen

Remember The 21 Day Fast

I also want to share with you the different things
like drinking water for two days, the next two days
eat fruit, then the next two days eat vegetables, then
go back to two days of water, two days of fruit, then
two days of vegetables. I believe it is called **_The Ta-
Ha Fast_**. By the time you go back to the water your
whole body makes a spiritual change. You must
remember the process is not complete until you do
this for 21 days. I know I should have put that first.
I'm just trying to explain to you several things about
how to eat to live. Learning these things is one of
the greatest gifts you can give to yourself; some of
the best of the teachings of The Honorable Elijah
Muhammad, and you can bear witness by what I'm
saying. He says it so simply and he makes it so
plain, and yet we hear it, but still many don't fully
understand. And the reason we don't understand it
is because we never follow through and take the
steps that he tells us to take. We may eat once a day,
and we just stop right there, and won't strive to eat
once every other day or every three days, and barely
can go on a fast when we're supposed to. We can't
just talk about life as if we we're like "bean soup

scientists" and fail to go through the steps that he is giving us, and expect proper results. As he plainly puts it, "do for self or suffer the consequences."

Just look at what's going on in the world. Obesity is running wild through our community. Lord knows what our children are eating to make them get so big. The hormones that they put in the foods, it's something that's not meant for humans. Anytime a 13 and 14 year old has the body of an adult, something is wrong with their diet. That's why it's so important to learn how to eat to live.

The best experiences that I've ever had was when I was practicing how to eat to live on a higher plain than once a day. I got up to eating every 3 days, 4th, 5th, 6th and finally stopped at 7. If I didn't do it, this book wouldn't exist. Although today I only eat once a day, in those days I had the zeal and youth to strive hard in it due to our spirit back then. What I'm saying is that sometimes you have something and you don't realize how valuable it is until it's not there anymore. You should know what I mean if you ever ran 8 miles and now can't even run 1 mile, or if you ran 20 miles and now you can't run 5 miles. You build yourself up to something and once you stop, you lose the discipline. It is easy to lose the discipline, and hard to get it back. What I'm sharing here is that which The Honorable Elijah Muhammad taught us was from God Himself, in the person of a divine man by the name of Master Fard Muhammad. We have something to be happy about for the rest of our lives.

If you have any kind of illness, from cancer to asthma, to heart problems, the antidote would be to get "How to Eat to Live" Book One and Book Two. If you ever want to look good, if you ever want to feel good, if you ever want to think well, work on the dietary law taught by The Honorable Elijah Muhammad.

Truthfully, I can't even express in words how good I felt eating once a week. We all have goals; we all have dreams, but you'll never know life until you practice what The Honorable Elijah Muhammad gave to us. These books "How to Eat to Live" Book One and Two, "Message to the Blackman", "Fall of America", "Our Saviour Has Arrived" are guidelines for our success. Please don't forget "The Holy Quran" and "The Muslim Daily Prayers" book. We have all of these beautiful books. I'm truly speaking what's in my heart.

Chapter Seventeen

1975: The Separation

When I came into the nation in 1972, I left in 1975 when The Honorable Elijah Muhammad was no longer in our midst. That's how I got away from the books. I give all praise and thanks to Allah for The Honorable Minister Louis Farrakhan for standing back up. When I saw him at Cornell University in 1977, he said to me, "I need your help" and of course I said, "Yes sir," but at the time I was not ready. I was ready to get me another shot of Johnny Walker Red! That was my god at the time. Just remember, the minister's wakeup call was Brother Jabril. He gave him the Quran and said read, now look at our leader. What I'm trying to say is look at our Nation. Whether or not you were present in the early years of the Nation, we weren't dying like we are dying today; it proves that we need the teachings of The Honorable Elijah Muhammad more now than ever before. How to Eat to Live. Most Muslims do not eat once a day. I don't want you to get my story twisted, but I'm going to speak as though somebody is interviewing me. "Do the Muslims look better now than they did then, Brother Joe?" I would have to say, "No. No they don't. They look like somebody who just got out of jail and don't get high." I'm not putting my Muslim brother down; I'm trying to uplift him. When you go to the hospital, most times they may have to hurt you in order to heal you; so if any of my words offend you, it's only because I love you and I love the Nation, and I know we don't have to live like this. What I mean is when you are incarcerated and you don't have access to the drugs, you begin to look better. When you're off of the drugs, the body begins to heal itself and you start to look better. We have to work on getting that distinguished look. You have to ask yourself why Muslims don't stand out like we used to in our appearance. We're not glowing. We have to get this back in full effect; then our love follows, our aura changes, and we learn how to talk to and treat our people better.

You may not realize it, but by **not** eating right, most of the time, we don't even sound the way a Muslim follower of The Most Honorable Elijah Muhammad should sound. We sound like lost-founds. We must get back to the dietary law. We get so emotional because we have eating problems; as if food is our god. I want to see everybody look different. We shouldn't have to wait until it's time to fast or when Ramadan comes up. Let's start counting our blessings. How would you know what I'm talking about if you never call on the God to connect you to what The Honorable Elijah Muhammad gave us? What I mean by blessing is, it's a blessing to have such a valuable book that could make a 50 year old look 30 years old if he's eating properly. If that's not a blessing, then what is a blessing? How many times have people asked your age and when you told them, they said that you don't look that age? That's a blessing! The Honorable Elijah Muhammad said that we could look 16! Count your blessings.

Take for instance a baby, a newborn. If you notice things about new babies, they don't start getting features and changing their looks until they start eating table food. Their table food tastes better than their regular food. It's just like breast milk. It may taste nasty to us but not to a baby; but we prefer cow's milk over breast milk because it tastes better to us. Just like saying looks can be deceiving, so can taste. Most of our people think that pork chops taste good, but it's not good for us. Chitterlings too. I know I'm putting things out there but I'm being real. Food is just like a drug because whenever we use something in excess, it becomes a drug. That's why many of us are obese from overeating. It's an old saying, "How to win a man's heart is through his stomach." Just mention food. The brothers and sisters will say, "Food? Free food??!"

Chapter Eighteen

Captain Yusuf Shah's Guidance

Another experience that took place before 1975 was when Brother Captain Yusuf Shah put us to an eating test by asking us questions. He was talking to about five of us. He asked, "Let's be honest, what do you eat first? The steak, the peas, the rice or the cabbage?" In other words, he was asking which do you eat first, the vegetables or the meat? I was straight up and said "the meat." The majority of us said the meat; But before we answered he said, "Now let's be aware of this question. I watch some of you eat so I know what y'all eat, so let's not start the lying." Then he said, "Dessert, I left that out. Do you eat your peaches, cake or apple sauce first?" So again my lying conscience clicked on and I thought, "He watches," so I said "dessert first." What was so amazing about Captain Yusuf Shah is that he was teaching me something I didn't read in "How to Eat to Live". What he was teaching me was how to eat properly. He said to us, "If you eat the meat first, the meat might be so good that you ask for another piece of steak or another piece of chicken. By doing this, your desire for eating the vegetables is not there because now you're full. That's why I asked y'all did you eat your dessert first. What I'm trying to break down to you is if you eat a bean pie, a bunch of candy or sweets first, by doing this you'll never be able to eat your vegetables. Actually you're spoiling your appetite, so it's always best to eat your vegetables first then your meat, then your dessert."

When you learn these kinds of things, it's very easy for you to start every other day, every three days, every two days, etc. It's like going through something. You know how they say, after the struggle of learning how to eat properly comes ease. I can gladly testify to how good I felt eating once a week. It was like I didn't have a problem in the world. I was so relaxed. When I was supposed to be sleeping, it seemed like I was just resting. When I was dealing with my brothers and sisters it took me a lot to get upset, because your mind is so calm. You're very open, so you'll notice if you have had a problem tolerating certain brothers or sisters that can say things to you that really upset you, it's easier now because although you are still vulnerable, you are more open minded.

Chapter Nineteen

<u>One Day A Week Journey</u>

As believers, we are to meet and overcome all
obstacles in our paths. Well, food is one of the
hardest obstacles. When you learn to overcome the
desire for food, you get a better understanding of
how your brothers and sisters struggle too. I like
what The Honorable Elijah Muhammad said, "I can
put you in heaven at once." I can clearly believe it
because I sho 'nuff was in heaven. I would just sit
and watch people eat and drink coffee or tea. At
times I could go to the juice bar and get me some
juiced carrots, beets, celery, and I'm straight. One
week I just drank blended apples, bananas and
other fruits. When I ate once a week and it was time
for my meal on Sunday, I would eat a salad. That
was my meal. I want you to clearly understand when
I say I ate once a week. When Sunday came, in the
morning I ate eggs, toast, hash browns. I know
what you thinking, "POTATOES?" But, don't forget,
I ate *once* a week, so potatoes couldn't do that much
damage to me. When you eat once a week your
stomach really shrinks down, so it's hard to sit and
eat just one single large meal. On Sunday, whenever
I was hungry, whenever I could get something in my

stomach, I ate a little more food. It's not that I ate all day, but that was my eating day. I tried to fill myself as much as possible before 12 o'clock a.m., because then I'm back on my journey. Then the process begins again and I won't eat again until the following Sunday. My discipline was so strong that most of the time Monday, Tuesday and Wednesday I didn't actually need the carrot or other juices.

One of the beautiful things I remember about eating once a week was going to The Juice Bar on 125th Street in Harlem. I used to go there since I didn't have my own juicer, but I realized that I was spending unnecessary money. One day while downtown on 14th St. and Union Square, I found a stand that sold fresh fruits and vegetables, so I bought a lot of it. The next time I went to The Juice Bar I brought my own fruits and vegetables with me. I held up the bags and asked the owner, "How much would you charge me if I gave you this to put in your juicer for me?" He looked at the giant bags and said "I could make a lot of cups out of that. I'll tell you what, you bring the stuff here and I'll do it for no charge because there'll be extras here for me. I gain and you gain." Then the brother asked me, "Brother Joe, can you get me the same connection?"

I said, "Can I still bring mines here?" He told me, "Brother, when you get me the connection you don't have to spend another dime here. Just come get your juices." It was so beautiful. I didn't have to spend nothing, he had it. Sometimes I would just stop in there with somebody else and he would just smile and ask "What do you want today, Brother Joe? How many juices do you want?" I was just smiling and I would tell him, "I'm alright today. I'm just here with my friend." He said, "It's an honor for me to supply you, not so much because you gave me the connection, but for just being able to look at a brother that could eat once a week, and I'm able to make your juices."

Chapter Twenty
<u>"Food God"</u>

Another thing I experienced when I was eating once a week was with our beautiful Captain Dennis Muhammad when he had his restaurant on 147th St & St. Nicholas. One day when I came into the restaurant, he was eating and he said to me, "Come here for a minute," and walked me out of the restaurant. I thought he wanted me to go on a run or had a detail for me to do. He reached in his pocket and pulled out some money and gave it to me. I said, "What is this for?" He said, "Brother Joe, get you some coffee or tea because I know you ain't gonna eat nothing, and drink it out here". He had an outdoor seating area. I said to him, "Why do I have to drink it out here, Brother Captain Dennis?" He said, "I will be honest with you. I'm eating me some steak and some other stuff. I don't feel comfortable with you around". I said, "I don't say nothing when people are eating." He then said, "I don't know if you know it or not, but you are a food god...you're a food god. If they don't know it, I know it, and it's very uncomfortable eating in front of a food god. Please Brother Joe, drink it out here." I just smiled. I'm not going to say that he souped me up, but yeah, my ego did swell up. He did more than souped me up, I had a swelled head. There I was, out there drinking my coffee. I was beyond souped up. What I learned from this is you must remember, words can make you feel up or down. He put a beautiful thought in my head and the swelling didn't come down for a couple of days. All praise is due to Allah. I didn't go around bragging because if you are really that good in something, all it does is humble you. Take for instance a martial arts master. We can use Brother Anthony in Chicago. You look at him, a humble brother, and would never know how dangerous he is. Also, take for instance The Honorable Minister Louis Farrakhan; you wouldn't even have a clue how awesome and fiery he is until when you push the wrong button.

So, I give all praise and thanks to Allah, who came in the person of Master Fard Muhammad for teaching and training The Honorable Elijah Muhammad for three and a half years. That's why we have to always say, "All praise is due to Allah." I can't say it enough. One of the most beautiful things that I hear The Honorable Minister Louis Farrakhan saying about Master Fard Muhammad is that he would climb a mountain 40 miles high just to teach and save one of us. He didn't say walk 40 miles, he used the word climb. Master Fard also said he would eat rattle snakes just to save one. Teaching us how to eat to live, we need to get back to this way of thinking as Muslims. This is 2012 and Muslims did not die like we're dying today. Muslims in the past did not look like we look today. I beg you, I plead with you not to underestimate the importance of eating to live.

Chapter Twenty One
<u>No Joke</u>

In my opinion and in my understanding, I could be 100% wrong, but many of our victories before 1975 is because we dealt differently with eating to live back then. Eating to live was strictly enforced and I will share an incident that happened to me to prove what I am saying to you. In 1973, me and another brother were coming from the Bronx after picking something up for Brother Minister James 7X. When we got back to Harlem, it was about 1 pm and we stopped off at the Steak N Take at 116th Street. The brother ordered some food to go and I placed an order too. Big mistake. Since my brother got his food first, he got dealt with first. Before we knew it, two other brothers entered the Steak N Take. I don't recall if they were Lieutenants or not, but these brothers walked over, and one of them started to question the brother that had gotten his food first. He said, 'Brother, are you on medication?' He said, "No, Sir." Then he asked, "Are you coming off of a fast? He said, "No, Sir." Then he said, "Do you eat once a day?" He responded, "No. No Sir." At this point the brother had heard enough. He said, "Brother, if you are not eating once a day, don't come out here in the daylight and shame yourself like this!" I knew I was getting dealt with next, so I didn't even stick around for my food and took off!

I stayed away from that restaurant for a while after that. When I went back to the Steak N Take about a month or two later, it was like the cooks had elephant memories. The brother remembered the earlier incident and how I left without my food and without paying. He looked at me and said, "Brother you owe!" I said,"Where's the food?" He said, "Don't play with me brother." It was strict, even if you were chewing gum, you got dealt with. You couldn't just do whatever you felt like doing. It was like what the Honorable Minister Louis Farrakhan would say, "That's the way it was."

We spent time together. A lot of us ate together at the same time. It was a spiritual thing. My God, that bean soup they used to make! I'm not gonna say they can't make bean soup like that anymore, but it was delicious. The toast that was made with bread from the Muslim bakery stood out. They even smoothed the butter on with something that looked like a miniature broom. There was nothing like it. I share all of this to say how much we've gotten away from the way things were. After being taught how to eat properly, now we eat just to eat. There's no discipline. We've got to do better.

Chapter Twenty Two

Captain Shah: It's The Glow Brother!

Some of the things that helped me to even get the thought of eating once a week were some of my past experiences in the Nation. In 1973, I recall selling "How to Eat to Live" Books One and Two at the corner of 125th Street and Lenox Avenue and Brother Captain Yusuf Shah came by smiling. He stood there watching me as he was smiling, so you know I had to ask him, "What are you smiling at?" He said, "You." Then I saw more than a smile, something was funny to him. He was now laughing. Something I was doing was funny to him, so you know, I had to ask, "Captain Shah, what's so funny about me?" He really started laughing then. I was having such a good time selling them, so I started laughing too. I didn't know why I was laughing but it was just a spiritual moment. As his laugh slowed down he said, "The funny thing about you, Brother Joe, is that you don't even know why you're selling those "How to Eat to Live" books so fast." My response was, "Because I'm a good salesman." Then he really started laughing. He said, "That's not why the books are flying out your hands." By then I was doing a little laughing and feeling a little silly because I didn't know why I was able to sell the books so fast, so I asked Captain Shah, "Why are they flying out my hands so fast?" He said, "I will tell you at dinner tonight." I had been down this road before with Captain Yusuf Shah. What I mean by this is the dinner; he wouldn't tell me right away, I would have to wait to find out.

It just happened to be Wednesday and that's the night I eat. I don't remember what month, but it was the summer. I met Captain Shah for dinner and I was anxious to find out why I was able to sell those books so fast. He didn't tell me right away, and he could see that I was waiting for his answer. After he kept me waiting long enough, I got the most beautiful answer. Captain Shah asked me, "Brother Joe, how often do you eat?" I said,"I eat Wednesday and Sunday, or it might even be Thursday and Sunday. It all depends on whether I have a real urge to eat on Wednesday, or else I can hold out until Thursday." I just want to remind you this was in 1973. This was not the year of my eating once a week. That thought was not yet in my head. He continued, "You have some beautiful skin and you're looking good, so the customers are looking at you selling the book "How to Eat to Live"and they see your glow and that beautiful skin and think to themselves, 'I gotta get me that book! Maybe that book will help me to look like that!" Well brothers and sisters, boy did I learn something that night! It got even better. It was the following Monday at FOI Class that the brother from California came to New York and taught on "How To Eat To Live." I told you that story earlier about meeting "another food scientist" who introduced me to the 21-day cleansing fast.

Chapter Twenty Three

<u>Captain Shah Teaches The Science of Drilling</u>

I want to share another beautiful experience I had with Captain Yusuf Shah. This took place at another dinner with him. I loved to drill and was very good at it. After we drilled one day, Captain Shah said I was great at drilling, but he wanted to explain something to me. He took me to dinner and with a smile on his face he said to me, "Brother Joe, you know how to drill but you don't have the jewel of drilling, the jewel of what you get out of it." Can you imagine knowing how to drill, and you're winning in drill competition, and yet don't even know whatcha got? While still eating dinner he said, "When the D.I. calls the drill you don't question the D.I. you just follow the order." He went on to explain it to me more, he said, "So now when you finish drilling and the lieutenant asks you to do something, even if you disagree, that gives you more reason to carry out the order and then be dismissed. You don't need to stay in his midst." So brothers and sisters what I learned is that drilling is practice to hear and obey; to follow orders and carry them out without questioning them, as long as it don't conflict with your religion. After he explained this, I began hearing and obeying, not just at drill.

A few days later I came to fully experience what Captain Yusuf Shah had told me when First Officer Richard 8X was arguing with another officer over me. When I went to Captain Shah and told him that they were almost fighting over me, he said they liked working with me because of my being able to hear and obey. Learning the beauty of hearing and obeying to this day helps me still.

Chapter Twenty Four

<u>What I Learn, I Share</u>

The Honorable Elijah Muhammad said, "My true followers eat once a day." If you don't eat once a day that don't mean that you not a follower, you're just not a **true** follower.

We must always remember Islam is our way of life. We talk it, we eat it, we drink it, we walk it, and we think it. Islam is love. We have to learn how to love to eat properly. God is love. It's hard to say we love one another and we're so quick to harm one another.

This is why eating to live is one of the most important things about our Islam. Eating right helps your spirit. It helps you feel rested because with eating right, you're not as tired as you usually would be. In some kind of way you gotta believe that food is a drug. You can feel it because when you eat you get drowsy. A person that constantly eats three, four, fives times a day is always tired. Look at the pressure that we're putting on our body. When we have food in our stomach and our stomach is working and working, and working, our mind cannot think right when it's time to make a decision.

It's easy for us to say I want to be in the hereafter, but how can we be in the hereafter if we're not eating right? You also have to realize we are gods; we're baby gods; so when are we going to start acting like gods? Most of our bad attitudes come from eating wrong. You are what you eat. It's not so hard to believe it if you constantly eat greasy, fried foods, and you're constantly eating a lot of potatoes and heavy meat.

We must realize that we are following a genius. I'm talking about The Honorable Elijah Muhammad and The Honorable Minister Louis Farrakhan. We're talking about geniuses. The Most Honorable Elijah Muhammad says think 5 times before we speak. Eating wrong makes you a liar. Come on let's keep it real. When someone asks you, "Aren't Muslims supposed to eat once a day, do you eat once a day?" It's easy for us to lie to them because we think we're superior to them. We got superior knowledge but we don't use it.

I have witnessed Muslims early in the morning eating coffee, muffins, donuts, eggs right in front of guests at the mosque. And the sad part about it is, we don't feel no shame. It's as though it's fair-seeming for us to carry on like this. Last Saviours' Day I saw a lot of believers in Mcdonalds.

FOI and MGT in McDonalds. Then we try to justify it. The Minister gets all kinds of reports. What we must realize is that discipline is an honor, and being disciplined does not mean that we are being punished. We are learning to obey those in authority even when they are not present. Even when Master Fard Muhammad, The Honorable Elijah Muhammad, and The Honorable Minister Louis Farrakhan are not present (but they are present) you have the Restrictive Laws, Conduct of a Muslim, "How to Eat to Live", and all of the other books. If you look into your heart with a positive mind, you have the ability to change your life in one day. But you can't always consistently show weakness. It's time to wake up black man and woman. When you hear your stomach growling you say to it, "You can growl all you want; you ain't getting nothing until the right time!" You can do it.

Chapter Twenty Five
We Dig Our Graves With Our Teeth

I'm sharing this with you because we're in some dark hours. The Minister said the majority of us are eating wrong. The Minister is teaching and we're cheering before we even finish hearing what he's saying, like we're in some kind of sugar fit. We must realize the path of wickedness and wrongdoing is as wide as the ocean. To do right is very narrow. Let me get right down to it. Whoever told you it was easy to be a Muslim told you a lie. It's hard to be a Muslim. One of the hardest parts of a Muslim's job, in all the laws, is how to eat to live. You might not know, but most of our problems and sickness come from eating all times of the night. Just picture that. We love eating more than we love trying to understand what The Honorable Elijah Muhammad is saying to us. Just take some pointers when The Honorable Elijah Muhammad said he chewed 22 times, some say 24 times, before he swallowed his food. Actually I can say to myself I may take a couple of bites and swallow. I don't know how to eat right, I'm still striving. It's so much. Like I said it's hard to be a Muslim. We still have our appetites, we still have our desires, but what causes these things? Bad habits! "I gotta have my coffee in the morning, I need my sugar." How to Eat to live.

Chapter Twenty Six

Wisdom

Now, I want to share some wisdom with you directly from "How to Eat to Live" Book Two that helped to strengthen me on my journey to eating once a week.

The following excerpt from "How to Eat to Live" Book Two by The Most Honorable Elijah Muhammad set the stage for my journey to eating once a week:

How to Eat to Live Book Two, page 182 (last paragraph)

"Only eat one (1) meal a day and you will surely live long. Eat the proper food if you eat once, twice or three times a week. Do not say that you cannot eat once a week. It is the way that you train your stomach. You can make a habit of eating once every week and you will survive happily. So, EAT TO LIVE and not to die."

Conclusion

We often fail to realize that when we process and graduate out of processing class, in reality we're really still processing. Life is a process. Life is always going to be good times and bad times, ups and downs, but we must realize we have the best teachings in the world, and in the Universe. Eating properly helps you with your spirit in dealing with people. Some of us eat right, but we have a problem with the way we treat people and handle one another. I can honestly see that some of us suffer with bad attitudes, and eating good food alone won't give you strength to change this within you. It's like a cancer. If your bad thoughts outweigh your good thoughts, it may be difficult to relate to your brother and to what I am trying to say here. Just look at the beautiful appearance we had taken on when The Honorable Elijah Muhammad started teaching us how to eat to live. I can't go back but too far, but we were beautiful. We were so beautiful but some did not realize how beautiful, and what Islam was doing for us too. When The Honorable Elijah Muhammad said,"*I will set you in heaven at once*", even today we still don't understand this. We have to ask ourselves why we are not in heaven; because we're not at peace mentally with one another. The Honorable Minister Louis Farrakhan recognized this and he gave us instructions to look into Dianetics and to study it's teachings on"auditing" and it's usefulness to help better our behavior towards one another. All of this, believe it or not, ties into how to eat to live. What I realize is that Dianetics cannot help you if your heart is not right. If we don't start purifying our heart towards one another, our beloved Minister Farrakhan proves right again. He said the majority of us are like Yacub's people. Just remember this: I'm not the one that said it, I'm only one who bears witness that what he said is true, because Yacub taught us to eat the wrong food and it made us other than ourselves. It's time for us to love again. Let's get back on our bean soup. I believe if we ate bean soup for one week it will clean out our system. Can't you believe, you have the power to read "How to Eat to Live" and change your appearance? We just don't stop there. Change our thoughts toward one another. Some of us were never taught how to love the teachings of The Honorable Elijah Muhammad. Excuse me; what I mean is that most of us were never taught how to love. We have lovely teachings but somehow we can't apply it to ourselves. I don't know why the teachings are so clear to me. I don't understand all that The Honorable Elijah Muhammad said in "Message to the Blackman", but he said something plain. When he said we are the best, the wise, but do not know it; some kind of way, we don't think this applies to us. We should want to eat right and to love right. We should want to be the best at loving one another. We should want to be the best in everything we do as long as it's right.

I love buying bean soup on Wednesday for the believers and guests, it makes me feel so good to see our brothers and sisters come to the mosque and enjoy themselves. I also enjoy feeding the homeless, and although everyone that comes is not homeless, I love feeding our people in general. An idea recently came to me that at my table on 127th Street I want to give away *free* bean soup once a week, that way I will be able to hand something to the people for their support. If you don't have the money for all the expensive food you would like to eat, the Honorable Elijah Muhammad taught us that we can live off of bean soup alone. If we tune in to "How to Eat to Live", that's just one portion of it. We have the power to change the world. Don't you want to change the world brothers and sisters? The Honorable Elijah Muhammad has a genuine love and concern for us, because look what he left us. Look at how we are blessed to have such a man as the Honorable Minister Louis Farrakhan. I live off of my brother's teachings. That's part of my business. I thank God for him. I love it when he talks about himself and when he says, "You don't know the man that walked five miles with holes in his shoes and used cardboard to keep the snow out." And he goes on to say, "You don't know the man that wore the same suit not for one year, not for two or three, but for 9 years." He also says, "I bought the suit from the Salvation Army". You have to ask, what kind of spirit did this man have in him? I pray to Allah to give me a small portion of what that man has. The lasting thought I want to leave you with is this; striving to eat and think right would also help us better our spirit. When we get into eating just anything, and at all times of the day, it will leave us with a bad spirit. We no longer have to ask ourselves why we look so bad and why we treat one another bad. When we're not eating right, we're definitely not thinking right, and if we're not thinking right we're not even striving to be a Muslim.

I'm quite sure I mentioned this before, and maybe we should do more research on what The Honorable Elijah Muhammad meant when he said, *"My true followers eat once a day."* What I got out of it is, when The Honorable Elijah Muhammad speaks, God is talking to us. He knows what he has is so divine, and he knows that we don't eat right. The Honorable Elijah Muhammad knows us like a book. When I hear of all the mad things that are going on, I just shake my head and thank Allah for The Honorable Elijah Muhammad. Imagine all that beautiful knowledge he gave to us and we're failing to apply it to ourselves. We could take a lesson from Curtis Mayfield's song lyric, "Educated fools from uneducated schools".

When our actions are out of line with the teachings of The Honorable Elijah Muhammad, that's not Muslim behavior. If Islam is our way of life, we eat Islam, we drink Islam, we talk Islam and we walk Islam. *It's our way of life!* The Honorable Elijah Muhammad; just sit and relax and think about him. You may not have ever met The Honorable Elijah Muhammad or perhaps you weren't a Muslim in that time but what he gave to me and the brothers and sisters that I learned from in the Nation of Islam is priceless!

This is Brother Joe, and *I am still here*. There are many that have tried to damage my spirit a many number of times throughout the years, but I thank Allah that through my experiences, I've learned not to be reactionary. This is the key. I was able to forgive with the peace of mind that I have gained from being in the Nation of Islam under the guidance of the Most Honorable Elijah Muhammad and the Honorable Minister Louis Farrakhan, especially through the teachings of prayer, fasting, and eating properly. Seek refuge in Allah from whatever afflicts you. Thank you for reading these words.

I am your brother,

As-Salaam Alaikum

About the Author

In 1955, the year that Minister Farrakhan began receiving his spiritual life from the Honorable Elijah Muhammad, Brother Joe was receiving his physical life. A native of the Bronx NY, when he was a little boy, the neighborhood preacher would come by to take him for walks around the community. Joe was always reaching out for people and would preach about loving one another. "The people would pick me up and kiss me." he recalls. "I was always a loving and giving person, I would give away things to my friends, not that I was trying to buy them, but I just always loved giving."

As a teenager, Brother Muhammad remembers being introduced to The Nation of Islam, "It was the best kind of love that I'd ever seen in any group of brothers and sisters." Being raised in New York had its influences on young Joe, with giants such as Malcolm X, Langston Hughes, James Baldwin, and the like all residing in the same community, "I remember being a little boy watching Minister Farrakhan on Channel 13. Whenever I saw him, I was always inspired. I would fight my older brothers and sisters from switching the channel just to watch him on TV. I loved his spirit."

Brother Joe joined the Nation of Islam in 1972, and incidently became a member at Mosque No. 7 under the Honorable Minister Louis Farrakhan, the man whom he had celebrated in his youth, along with his legendary pioneer, Captain Yusuf Shah, until 1975. Currently a brother in good standing in the NOI, Brother Joe's unique oratory skills will find a way into even the youngest child's heart, as he continues to teach the youth in his community in Harlem, New York where he resides with his family.

Don't forget to Subscribe to

"THE FINAL CALL"
NEWSPAPER

Get your copy today!!!

Made in the USA
Middletown, DE
02 October 2017